This Poetry Book

Poetry Book #1

Claire Annabel

Made with ❤ on the BookLeaf Publishing Platform
www.bookleafpub.in
www.bookleafpub.com

Dedication

For those who believe they can't write poetry
Don't give up

Preface

Poetry is not my strong suit. In fact, it's something I don't do very often. I'm a Story writer and a Lyricist; but I still write Poetry when I feel the need.

These 21 poems in this book I feel show that. Poetry is not easy by any means, but it is still a beautiful form of writing. There is no overall theme to these poems. I let the poems come to me, just like how I do with all my writing, and what is in these pages is exactly that; words that came to me in a string of sentences that hopefully make as much sense to you as they do to me

Thank you for taking a read. I hope you enjoy them

Acknowledgements

Bookleaf Publishing - Thank you for presenting this opportunity to write a poetry book in a very short amount of time. It was a fun challenge and I hope this is something you continue to do for a long time

1. The Typewriter

The typewriter writes the story,
Like a Secretary,
It hangs on to every word being passed down
By its Boss

It creates its own music,
Setting the mood of every strike and slide
It could hold its own against a piano
If it wanted to give it a try

It may not be high speed,
Or need to be charged on repeat,
But like a human, it bleeds
And it bleeds all its sweat and tears into the words on
the pages,
to create something magical

And that is what gives the typewriter life

That gives the typewriter the strength that it needs
To continue being unique

2. Colors

Purple shades of Lavender
Golden shades of Yellow
Bring out this marvelous beauty,
Don't you think so?

Crimson shades of Red
Brown shades of Hazelnut
Every time I look at you
My heart wants to combust

Hunting for the darkest shades of Green
Mixing with the brightest Sky shades of Blue
My love for you is as due North as this sail,
It is as true as it is brought to you

Don't let the Jet Black of the night fool you,
It's always a misunderstanding color,
This ray is actually a rainbow of colors,
To show my undying love for you

3. Resisting You

Lingering touches
Stolen glances
That's as far
As we're willing to go

Nothing has been spoken
But the silence speaks so loud
This tension we've been feeling
Could knock us down

We're pulled to each other
Like moths to a flame
Gravitating towards each other
Without being able to place blame

The closer we get
The harder we resist
When all we want to do
Is embrace each other in a kiss

4. Target

Something was brewing
This I knew for sure
You could feel it
You could sense it
You could feel it to your core

Whisperings have been going around
But only to a select few
So unless you were in the know how
You wouldn't hear the news

"There's a target! There's a target!"
What did you just say?
Is someone trying to pick a fight
Out of the dead of night?

There's a Battle brewing here,
This I can confirm
The Target is being framed
And whoever believes it

Ought to be ashamed

Those 'Warriors' seem to think
The Target is as guilty as they say
They will come up with anything
Just to attach his name

Attack upon attack
Blow upon blow
They're not letting up
Not even to say hello
Lie upon lie
They stack up so high
How far do you think they'll get
Before the well runs dry?

"The target is safe!"
Well that's a relief
I know I've done my best
To give their lies a rest

This Battle they have raised
Is only the beginning
You see, I don't let anyone
Attack mon amour
So if you plan on taking the Target down
You better plan on there being a War

5. Sleepless Nights

Dreams don't come to me
I'm too tired for them now
I also haven't slept so soundly,
Since you stopped coming around

I keep denying you're the cause for my problems
Surely, one human couldn't possibly destroy my sleep?
Why would it even matter?
You said so yourself,
You don't need me

This is becoming silly
Maybe it's because I'm tired?
If you don't need me,
I sure don't need you
Isn't that how it's supposed to work?
I'm pretty sure
But I'm beginning to have doubts

Maybe I should talk to someone

Maybe they can make this make sense?
But I don't want to talk about this to anyone
It will only make the tears I can't keep at bay,
Become a harsh waterfall down my face

So it's settled, right?
You don't need me
And I sure don't need you
You're not the cause for my sleepless nights
And I'm pretty sure
I'm alright

6. Every Once In A While

Every once in a while, you cross my mind
The reason is always random
I don't enjoy it.
I don't want to think about you
I don't want to think about us
I don't want to think about how things were
I don't want to think about everything you said and done
to me
I don't want to think about it
I don't want to remember it
I don't want to feel the tinge of sadness
When I do
I don't want to think of you ever
You don't deserve to have even an ounce of my attention

Every once in a while, you cross my mind
Words upon words I should have said to you,
Come up out of the dust,
Wanting to finally be expressed
And no matter how many times

I write it down,
It doesn't seem to be enough
The words come back every time
The words of making you face,
What you did to me
Making you face,
Who you really are
They're written down
In so many forms,
But it seems they want to be spoken
And not just words

Every once in a while, you cross my mind
The feeling that this isn't over,
Crashes into me
I don't enjoy it.
I hope it's not true
I do not want you back
Or maybe I do?
Maybe it's the old me talking
You were not the best for me
I am free of you
Or am I?
If I look back, I see the progress I've made
You no longer have a hold on me and I feel strong; I can
breathe
But when I face forward,

I get hit with just how much damage I still have to repair
And I feel tired, weak; like this is never going to end

Every once in a while, you cross my mind
And I struggle to not let what you did
Effect me
Effect others
Turn me into someone I'm not
Have your red flags be found in someone else

You cross my mind
And I wonder if I cross yours
And if you remember
All the things
You did to me too

7. Dreaming of You

Dreaming of you is a treat
It's becoming rare
To see you in my sleep

Dreaming of you is a pleasure
The moments we share
Keeps getting better

Not dreaming of you is a nightmare
I search for you in every corner
And wonder what I did to deserve
This kind of horror

When I wake up,
I don't want to
I want to be back with you
And not alone in my room

What can I do
To make you come back?

Other than stay in this bed
And will dreams of you to circle back

8. The Outsider

On the outside looking in
I see people happy
They are smiling and laughing with each other
They're holding hands
They're pecking lips
They're sitting together on that bench
Why haven't I been let in?

On the outside looking in
People pass me to enter the sphere
Instantly paired up with their forever love
I try banging on the dome
But no one hears me
Why haven't I been let in?

I meet different people on the outside
Some I fancy in that light
But then, something changes in their eyes
And I'm alone on the outside once more
What is it I'm doing,

To not be able to cross that line?
Or is there something I'm not doing,
That is keeping me in the shadow of night?

Person after person walks through that veil,
And I still have yet to get through
Why haven't I been let in?

On the outside looking in
It's hard not to feel blue
I watch in misery
As everyone I know
Gets to have what I want most

Am I trying too hard to find love?
Or am I too hard for someone to love?
These questions in my head
Swirl through my mind

As another year goes by
It's getting harder to believe
That I will be walking through that veil
And have that sweet victory

I don't know how much longer
I can go on
It's getting harder to watch

The pain is too strong
There's nothing I can do
I'm stuck here
On the outside looking in

9. Walls

I can feel you, but I can't see you
I'm staring at this wall
It's big, it's long
There's no end in sight
But I can feel you from the other side

I bang on the wall
There's a faint bang echoing back to me
A sense of relief rushes through me
I look around and grab a hammer and chisel
Beginning my work of trying to make this wall
disappear

With each line of cement that's cleared,
The bricks fall with a violent smack to the ground
As gravity helps me take it down

Once a few bricks are removed
I look through the hole at the view
And to much anguish

I see another layer staring back at me

I knew breaking through your walls would entail
Me being as patient and persistent as I'm willing to be
From the anguish, determination shines through
And I start to work on the next wall to get to you

10. Not In The Cards

Maybe I should sleep on this
Maybe I shouldn't be thinking about it
But I fought too hard
I fought for so long
Giving up
Is not in the cards

I may want to stop trying for the night
I may want to quit altogether
But something in me says it's not right
To give up something
That you treasure

11. Fighting It

Being below the radar
Is exactly where we want to be

We exchange glances when others turn away
We pretend we don't feel anything
When the attention is on us

Things slip here or there
We both know what the other is thinking
We both know what the other wants
We gravitate to each other like magnets
How has no one figured us out?

When we're alone, that's when the true intimacy
happens
The light touches
The lingering stares
Why do we fight it?
We both know what the other wants
Why do we keep fighting it?

Or is this all in my head?
Am I just imagining this is happening?
Now you're coming closer
This is new
Your hand brushes over mine

No, this isn't all in my head
So why do we keep fighting it?
Why do I keep fighting it?

12. Shine

You need to believe in yourself a little more
Bring out that confidence
You hide in your unsure

You're so silent in that way
If anyone where to explore your depths
They would be shocked at what lays
Behind those walls of yours

Now is your time to shine
Show them why you claim the light
Now is your time to shine
Show them how it's done right

13. I Am Ready

I am ready
I am ready for this to happen
I am ready for my dreams to come true
I am ready for that prolonged success

I am ready
I am ready for finally reaching my goals
I am ready for the sun to shine down on me
I am ready for a love to swallow me hole

I am ready
I am ready to be given that chance
I am ready for someone to see the best in me
I am ready for that change

I am ready
I am ready to walk out of the shadows
I am ready to live my best life
I am ready to go on adventures
I am ready to see the sunrise

I am ready to fly
I am ready to trust you
I am ready to dance like no one's watching
I am ready to be the best version of myself
I am ready to go into the unknown

I am ready

14. Heart to Heart

Heart to heart
We let this fall apart
It wasn't intentional
But now we are at different sides of the tide

Heart to heart
We tore each other apart
Words swung like weapons
Tempers ran high
Walls raised up to the sky

Heart to heart
We are at the destruction
It wasn't intentional
We hurt each other so much

Heart to heart
Our heavy feet meet in the middle
We face each other with our wounds blown open
We see each other for who we are

Heart to heart
We put down our weapons
We surrender to each other
Encompassing the other in protection
We understand each other a little more now
As we help heal the wounds
That were hiding behind the armor
We finally removed

15. Push

I push people away
It's what I do
I push and push and push
And they don't even try to stay

I lay everything on the line
They say They do too
Then I push at them,
To really see if they're telling the truth

You came into my life
So I pushed at you too
But just like a ball,
You bounced back into my arms

Now I'm standing here
Not knowing what to do
Because I never expected
For you to stay in the room

16. Light and Dark

The lights are on
But it's still black as night
How can that be
When the flames are burning bright?

Is this an illusion?
Is it completely dark?
Will I find my way out of this?
Is there an end in sight?

Now it's too bright
Can someone turn down the light?
What is with these opposites?
What ever happened to balances?

There's got to be a way
To have the Day and Night coexist
If the Sun and Moon can do it
Surely these two sides can too

I've been told it's what you feed it
As to which side takes over
But I haven't been told what happens
If you don't feed either side
And they become out of control
With the hunger for attention taking over

17. This Poem

I'm trying to find inspiration to write this poem
I can't even think of a rhyme
That will hopefully make it sound like a wind chime

It's a shame really
Who would have thought coming up with a couple lines
That wove together so seamlessly
Would end up putting me at a lost for words
And have me be misunderstood?

Should I write about rain?
Should I write about distain?
What about autumn sunsets?
Or leaves flowing through the wind?
I could write about walks
But that would be a short talk

I'm no Dr. Seuss
So I'll keep thinking

But hopefully I can come up with something soon
Preferably before noon

18. Undercover

Undercover
That's where I need to live
That's where I need to stay

Their watching me
I feel like I can't let my feelings show
It's becoming impossible to not let go

You feel it too
I can tell by the way you move
You know they're watching you, too
You are undercover with me
Doing your best to not make a scene

Our secret hideaway
You can be you
And I can be me
We don't have to hide anymore
Behind closed doors

It's becoming nonsense
We shouldn't have to hide
What we are feeling inside

But it continues
We keep each other away from prying eyes
In order to protect what we're keeping inside
In order to protect what they would try to destroy
If they knew
There was something going on that they would
disapprove

19. Being Free

I watch from the sidelines
Seeing this game being played
I try to say something
But I get ignored

I watch in this silence
As people talk for me
I do have my own voice
When can I be free?

Decisions get made for me
I'm beginning to not know what I want anymore
I need to stop this madness
This can't continue
It's spiraling out of control
I need to open the door

With shaking knees, I stand
I walk away from the sidelines
I'm tired of waiting

I'm tired of being spoken for
This is my stance
Of finally being free

20. Deep Down

Deep down I know
I care for you
I know that part of my frustration
Is you

You drive me crazy
But deep down I know
I couldn't live without you

We may bicker
We may walk away
But we always come back to each other
I don't know what I would do without you
Because deep down I know
I love you
And deep down you know
You love me too

21. Love Is

Love is a trust fall
You don't know if you're going to be caught
Odds are suppose to be evenly split
But it seems like it's hardly in your favor

Love is a Free Spirit
It's not forced
Sometimes it doesn't stay
But when it finds its home,
The fire in it can keep one warm
Until their very last day

Love is kindness
There's a reason why
Its opposite is Hate
And why there is a thin line between the two

Love is the reason you see a range of colors
Love is the question and the answer

Love is behind everything I do
Because Love is everything I see in you